The
Water
Flower

The
Water
Flower

The Journey of a Lotus Seed

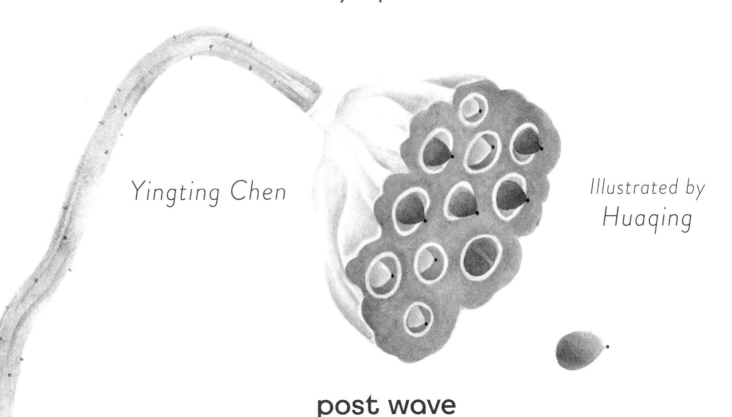

Yingting Chen

Illustrated by
Huaqing

post wave

Splash!

Autumn arrives, and a little lotus seed drops into
the water and drifts into a long, peaceful sleep.

But soon enough, Spring is here.

Crack!

The seed wakes from its slumber. Its hard shell splits open and the tiny tips of young leaves poke out, straining to break free.

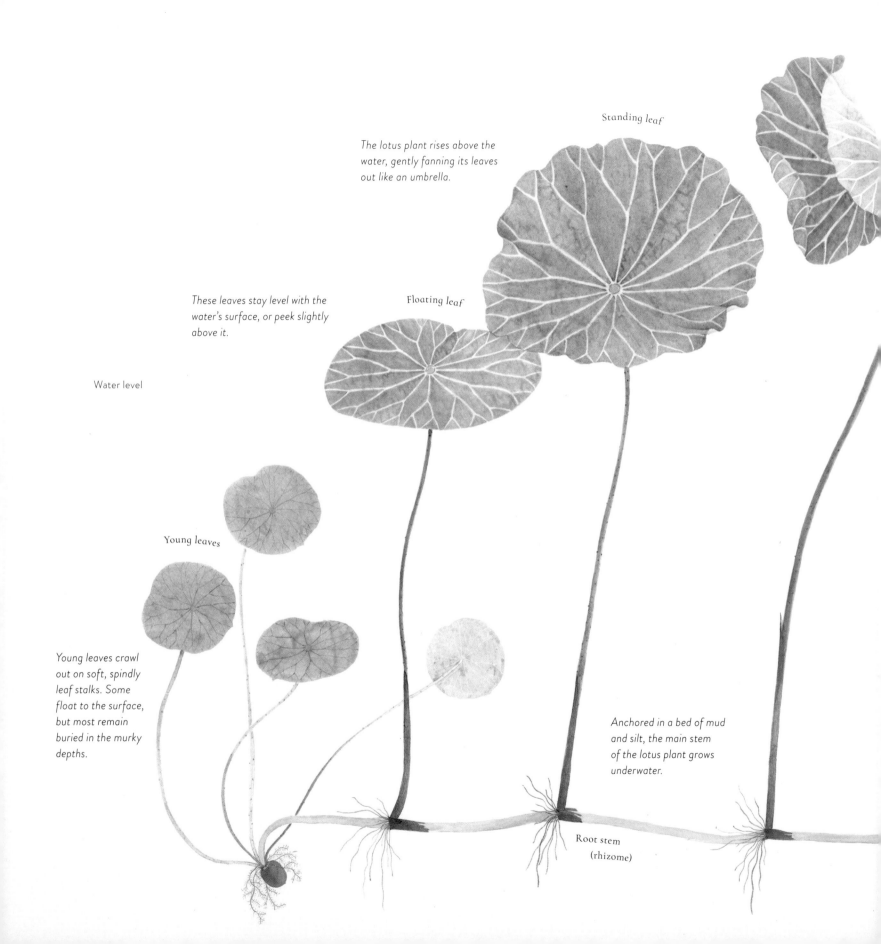

Standing leaf

The lotus plant rises above the water, gently fanning its leaves out like an umbrella.

These leaves stay level with the water's surface, or peek slightly above it.

Floating leaf

Water level

Young leaves

Young leaves crawl out on soft, spindly leaf stalks. Some float to the surface, but most remain buried in the murky depths.

Anchored in a bed of mud and silt, the main stem of the lotus plant grows underwater.

Root stem
(rhizome)

The growing bud stretches forward, pulling with it a long, thin stem from within the seed. It stretches higher and higher, sprouting leaves along the way – the race is on to be the first to break the water's surface.

Leaf bud

The growing lotus leaf curls in on itself like a tube, tapering at the sides. This helps the leaf to shoot upwards.

As spring turns to summer, the first leaves lift their heads above the muddy water. Held aloft by strong, sturdy stems, they soak up the glorious sunlight.

Gases, like oxygen and carbon dioxide, enter the leaf through tiny holes called stomata. The biggest one is in the middle of the lotus leaf, helping the plant to breathe.

The top of the leaf has tiny waxy hairs that make it waterproof. Water forms little beads that skate off the surface, keeping the leaf clean and dry.

Lotus bud

Flower bud

Sheaths are protective structures in plants. The lotus plant has two types: one to protect young leaves, and one to protect growing buds.

Most plant roots grow at the base of the stem, but lotus roots grow from specific points called nodes along their root stem.

Leaf sheath

Root

Bud sheath

The back of the lotus leaf looks lighter than the front because it holds more gas. This extra gas helps the leaf float and reflects sunlight, making the back appear brighter.

Early summer creeps in, and the air warms with anticipation. At the foot of a standing leaf, the first precious flower bud emerges. It drinks deeply, absorbing the rich nutrients delivered by green leaves and roots.

Patiently, it waits for the perfect moment to bloom.

Dawn breaks on the first day, and the flower bud swells.
A small opening appears. In the afternoon, it closes again,
as if nothing has happened . . .

On the second morning, the petals stretch, releasing a delicate fragrance. By late afternoon, they close again.

Corolla

The corolla, which is the group of petals on the lotus flower, opens at sunrise and closes at sunset. This helps keep the inside of the flower warm, attracting insects by offering a cozy shelter.

On the third day, the flower yawns open, unfurling its inner petals. By evening, it tries to gather them back, but no longer has the strength to fully close.

As the petals unfurl to the rhythm of the sun, the lotus flower's pistils and stamen mature. Bees buzz about, feasting on the flower's sweet nectar. They brush against the lotus's stamen and a sprinkling of pollen sticks to their hair. This fine powder is then carried from flower to flower, helping new seeds to grow.

Pistil

Stamen

The lotus flower closes for the night and quietly traps a bee within its petals. The bee waits patiently until dawn, then quickly makes her escape, fluttering free as the flower blooms open again.

By the fourth day, the lotus
flower flops open in exhaustion.
It will not close again.

Gently, the first petal tumbles
down into the water.

One by one, the lotus petals
droop, wither, and fall away . . .

The lotus root resembles a tree's trunk.
Branches grow from nodes along the
trunk, sprouting in different directions.

Only one leaf and one flower
can grow from one node.

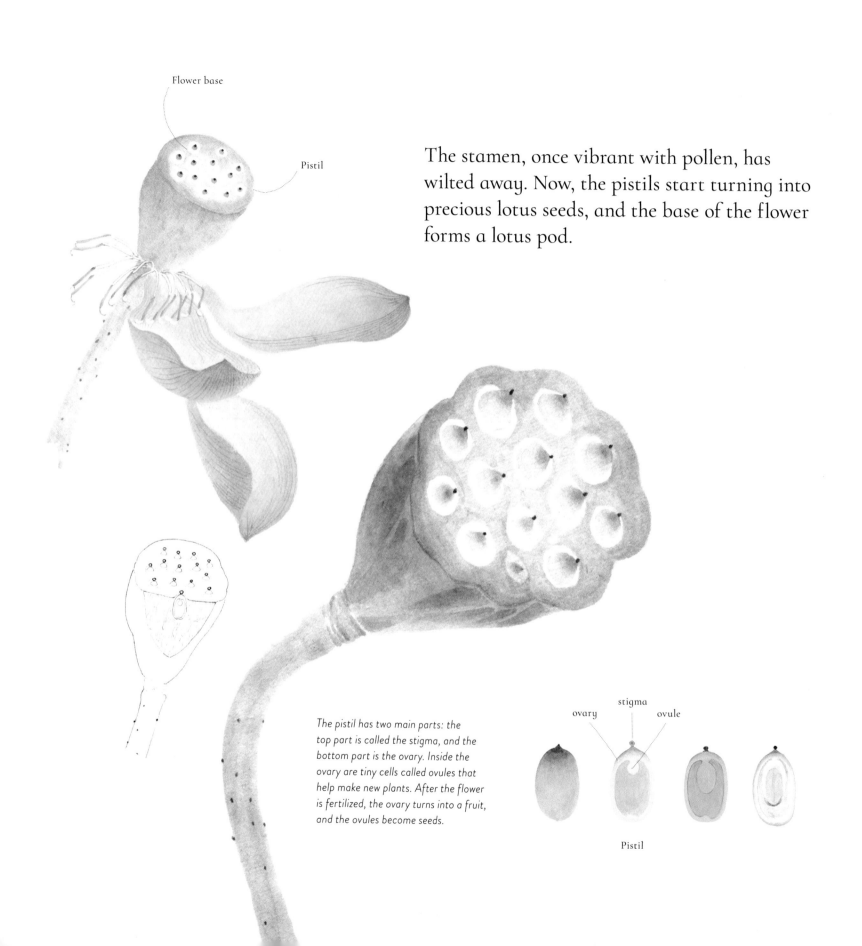

Flower base

Pistil

The stamen, once vibrant with pollen, has wilted away. Now, the pistils start turning into precious lotus seeds, and the base of the flower forms a lotus pod.

The pistil has two main parts: the top part is called the stigma, and the bottom part is the ovary. Inside the ovary are tiny cells called ovules that help make new plants. After the flower is fertilized, the ovary turns into a fruit, and the ovules become seeds.

ovary   stigma   ovule

Pistil

Lotus pod and seeds

The pod will hold and
protect the seeds inside.

Inside the seeds, there is
new life waiting to grow.

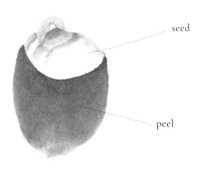

seed

peel

nut

nut cross-section   seed coat

embryo

seed leaves

young
seed leaves

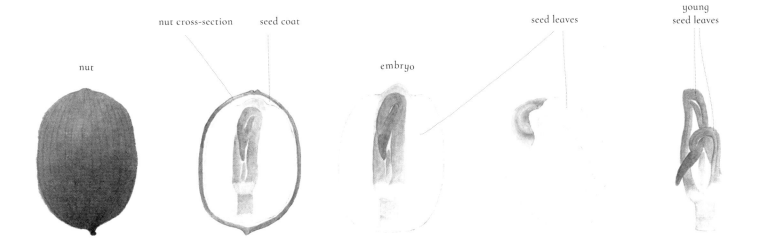

*Tucked safely away, the embryo
is the most important part of the
seed. This young, immature plant
will go on to form the next
generation of lotus flowers.*

*There are two 'seed leaves,' which
can store and transform nutrients
to help the embryo.*

Rear handle leaf

Terminal leaf

Lotus root harvesters call the
last tall, big, strong leaf at
the end of the lotus root the
'rear handle leaf.'

The short, small, weak leaf
that appears after the rear
handle leaf is referred to as
the 'terminal leaf.'

Lotus rhizome node

With each autumn rain, a chill arrives. The flowers and leaves wither, leaving only a few lotus pods on the water's surface. The lotus burrows into the mud, developing its first rear handle leaf. It transfers nutrients to the root stem, which grows plump to survive the coming winter.

The lotus plant has many 'pipes' inside it that carry air. These pipes go up to the leaves and flowers and down to the roots. They let oxygen from the water's surface travel through the plant, helping the lotus breathe and grow without suffocating in the water.

The nights grow longer and colder. The dried lotus pod embraces the lotus seeds, before bidding farewell and falling away.

Splash!

A lotus seed drops into the water and drifts into a long, peaceful sleep . . .

As spring arrives again, the little seed stirs . . .
ready to begin its journey anew.

Published in the USA in 2025 by Post Wave Children's Books,
an imprint of Post Wave Publishing UK Ltd.
Runway East, 24–28 Bloomsbury Way, London, WC1A 2SN
www.postwavepublishing.com

First edition 2021

Published with permission of Post Wave Publishing China
Original title: *Yi ke lian zi de sheng ming lü cheng* (一顆蓮子的生命旅程)
Written by Yingting Chen
Illustrated by Huaqing
Translated by Adam Casciaro & Liu Yinan

Copyright @ Post Wave Publishing China, Beijing, China 2021
www.hinabook.com

Library of Congress Cataloging-in-Publication Data is available

1 2 3 4 5 6 7 8 9 10

ISBN: 979-8-89509-011-4

Printed and manufactured in China by Leo
Paper Products, Heshan, Guangdong. Dec 2024

FSC
www.fsc.org

MIX
Paper | Supporting
responsible forestry
FSC® C020056